ANOTHER RUSSIA

ANOTHER RUSSIA

Through the eyes of the new Soviet photographers

From the Collection of
Daniela Mrázková and Vladimír Remeš

Introduction by Ian Jeffrey

Facts On File Publications
New York, New York · Oxford, England

Half-title: Lyalya Kuznetsova, Ural'sk, 1981
Title-page: Aleksandras Matsiyauskas, from the cycle
''Village markets'', 1972–84

© 1986 Daniela Mrázková and Vladimír Remeš
Introduction © 1986 Ian Jeffrey
Illustrations © 1986 the individual photographers listed opposite
First published in the United States in 1986 by
Facts on File, Inc.

Library of Congress Cataloging-in-Publication Data

Another Russia.

    Bibliography: p.
    1. Soviet Union—Description and travel—1970–
Views. I. Mrázková, Daniela. II. Remeš, Vladimír,
DK18.5.A56   1986   779'.9947085   86–6341
ISBN 0-8160-1553-8

Printed in Japan

10 9 8 7 6 5 4 3 2 1

Contents

Introduction by Ian Jeffrey

Many of our ideas about life in the modern USSR come from vintage imagery of power stations on the Dnieper, blast furnaces at Magnitogorsk and oil installations at Baku. In the great inter-war pictorial surveys, Buryat camel-masters and Bokharan carpet-makers rub shoulders with collectivized tractor drivers and industrial experts, researching, supervising and adjusting. In the most impressive of these early pictures young workers and the leaders of shock brigades appear as shining ideal types in such documentary surveys as *The Land Without Unemployment* by Ernst Glaeser and F.C. Weiskopf, published outside the Soviet Union in 1931.

At first glance, some of the photographs that appear in the present book evoke those heroic ideal types of the 1920s. Algimantas Kunchius's statuesque woman outlined against a clearing sky (*opposite*) might, in her day, have gained credit in the work of the shock brigade. But Antanas Sutkus's sensitive young pioneer looks altogether too apprehensive to have made much of a mark in the early days. And Sutkus's pair of veterans have been caught by fatigue and by the years. In the 1920s everything was still to do; this USSR, by contrast, has done its work and gathered memories and second thoughts along the way.

The photographs shown here provide, then, an opportunity for a new view of life in the Soviet Union. The earliest surveys concentrated single-mindedly on steel production, welfare and all the other elements which go to make up a flourishing modern society. Daily and private life hardly entered in, at a time of looking to the future. In this collection, by contrast, the texture of Soviet daily experience can be felt everywhere. These photographers open doors and presume an interest in the here and now. They can be prolific, even encyclopaedic. Aleksandras Matsiyauskas's Lithuanian markets, with their cattle, grain, pigs, poultry, stove doors and wooden figurines, teem with durable country life. Lyalya Kuznetsova's nomad tents are as profuse. Lithuanians barter, nomads feast, and weekend Russians honour their ancestors in labyrinthine cemeteries. It is a Russian custom to visit and to share a meal among the dead – but who until now thought that poignancy worth remark? Yet despite this evidence of traditional and of private life this is still evidently the USSR, a society with visionary notions. Just as Sutkus's veterans recall an earlier heroism so Boris Mikhajlov's part-time lady gymnasts keep in play an idea of human perfectibility. And Vladimir Siomin's sympathetic workers taking a break from the Trans-Siberian are pioneers for all that. Through this unglamorous naturalism these photographers keep the ideal in mind as an absence or memory.

89

92,93

38–41

Opposite:
Algimantas Kunchius, from the cycle 'Village Sunday', 1975–85

'Leader of a shock brigade of the Komsomol (Young Communists)', from Ernst Glaeser and F.C. Weiskopf, *The Land Without Unemployment* (1931)

Paradigms of femininity and labour may be disputed and qualified, but at the same time they are retained and renewed.

These photographs might also be read for their incidental details and small revelations, for Soviet doors are not readily opened. Notice, for example, the chess champion among that row of worthies behind Mikhajlov's lady exercisers, and 65 notice too that there are as many women as men in that local hall of fame. These details, over the nailed pinewood slats, suggest that the heroic shock brigaders of the 1920s laboured to good effect, and that disinterested brain work has an honoured place in Soviet life. On the other hand there are evidences of an unmitigated ordinariness in ordinary life, in Aleksandr Slyusarev's summer 17 commuters waiting on a platform like an upturned table top, and in Vyacheslav 136 Tarnovetskij's empty market site with its improvised water supply. And there are pieces of anthropological and folklore data, in the shape of Sutkus's new boy with a 94 leafy branch on his first day at school, and his line of country women keeping their 95 shoes safe from the roughness of the path.

The ordinary life celebrated here may have its framework and traditions, but above all it has a texture and a taste. Appetite, as feasting or, more humbly, as eating, drinking and smoking, is a subject and an end in itself in these pictures. What is evoked, recurrently, is the flavour of particular moments as, for instance, Kunchius's villagers respond to music, summer air and the sea, or Kuznetsova's 139 diners pause appreciatively over the remains of a meal. These are epicurean 56 photographers, devotees of touch and taste, and in this respect are free from those reformist and utopian impulses which have shaped so much of American as well as Soviet photography from the 1920s onwards. They observe, describe and appraise, and bring the place to a kind of piquant life which it has never had before.

Aleksandras Matsiyauskas, from the cycle 'Village markets', 1972–84

Despite documentary interludes this Soviet Union is an imaginary land, although so for that matter was the original foundation. But where the original dream was collective, modernist and prescriptive, these new imaginings of the 1970s and 80s are restorative, full of the weight and aura of the place. This re-working extends even to portrayals of the highest of Soviet achievers. In Mikhajlov's hall of fame and local gymnasium the portrait style is objective to the point of plainness, more Roman republican than romantic. By contrast, Anatolij Garanin's contemporary cast of virtuosi, directors and presidents are inward and intense, living in some state of flickering concentration impinged on by the taste of smoke. Although Garanin may be a respected official photographer, the implications of his work are personal rather than public. Together with the brooding private portrait of Boris Savelev by Elena Darikovich these dark images express an idea of the melancholy humour and of genius.

Garanin's are no ordinary portraits. At first sight they have the darkness and intensity of romanticism, but with an important supplementary element in that they are of smokers and in that respect refer to taste, touch and mortality. He can be thought of, with justification, as a melancholic artist for he links ideas of genius and inspiration with commonplace sensory evidence. The melancholic temperament was, in the psychology of the Middle Ages and after, especially associated both with genius and with sensuous baseness. Its element was the earth and its planet was Saturn, and although it soon came to be no more than a metaphor did such justice to art's sense of the transcendental hidden in the material that its force and fitness have never diminished. If, like his heroes and heroines, Garanin works under the sign of Saturn, Soviet photographers, and the culture at large, began under Jupiter, the orderly, lucid god, sanguine in temperament. Certainly, early Soviet photography, with its devotion to health centres, combine harvesting and factory building, deliberately eschews mystery and the dark side of mankind.

The melancholic artist lives among the stuff of the world, yet at the same time, through insight or influence, has access to or inklings of a truth which lies beyond appearance. Such an artist recognizes an imbalance between what can be seen and what can be sensed, and the result most often is an art of signs, a transitive art to be read through to an absent cause. Two of the most interesting artists here, Elena Darikovich and Boris Savelev, play this game of signs throughout. Savelev is pictured, or has himself pictured, as a watcher through a screen, which action hints at the difficulties of seeing and even suggests an idea of an objectless or internal vision. All of Darikovich's subjects lie elsewhere, disclosed only by traces, pointers or reflections. Except in the case of that model, modern town seen over what looks like a crude cemented dais she is not specific about elsewhere, whereas for her associate, Savelev, it is constituted of light, sound and energy, to be identified from their residues. He is on record as admitting to an interest in Eugène Atget, and his work, as represented here, constitutes a critique of the French artist's preoccupation with significant fragments. Where Atget elaborated, Savelev contradicts. Atget reflecting on water might bring together a well head, a down spout, a wooden barrel and a dipper; Savelev, by contrast, alludes to light in the form of a tipped, cast-iron standard, or as trapped, numbered and stoppered in

9

a rugged block, and then again as a shaky motif near to some isolated, geometrical 8
samples of the product itself. His closest contemporary is the American photogra- 5
pher William Eggleston, author of *The Georgia Project*, in which such large ideas
as light, decay and landscape are summarized and expressed heraldically in
coloured motifs: change, for example, seen twice over in the ruins of a building
rusted into autumnal tints, or the varied browns and blues of earth and sky shaped
and intensified in the costume of a child playing in the street.

Where the photographer Savelev has light and sound as his subjects, the
physicist Tarnovetskij tries to find a form for consciousness itself, for elsewhere
considered as Another. It would be difficult to imagine a more softly-spoken art or
one in which less of consequence happens. The old man in the market may have
been surprised, or just disturbed working at the sort of cleaning and sweeping job 136
which can often be more like reverie than labour. A woman and man on the edge of
a quiet lake or inland sea are no more than familiar, their tranquillity matched by 139
sunlight on a wall and the even ratios of the photographer's arrangement.
Companionship and a sort of mild discomfort are his other subjects, expressed
with extraordinary finesse. Photography, despite its objective capacities, has
never been put to this sort of use before; its adepts, if intent on society and
humanity, usually look for unmistakable signs of the times, for strong material. If
this photographer is to be compared with anything it can only be with that Russian
story writing which has mood and impulse in mind, where nothing is resolved,
where tomorrow holds more of the same. Tarnovetskij's discreet citizens might
have stepped from one of Vasily Shukshin's pages, or passed by in the
background. He has been quoted as saying, 'I take photographs of everything
because everything is part of my life', which sounds like the voice of an artist
keeping quiet, keeping the thread intact.

Tarnovetskij shows the lovers, or friends, living equably in an equable space by
the sea. After that sort of intimation of order there can only be disruption and a
falling short. It would be interesting to see how he deals with the Fall into society
and temporality, or if these pictures are part of some wider, larger project. Lyalya
Kuznetsova is one artist who more than touches on these issues. At one level she,
like Mikhajlov, is a documentary analyst capable of disclosing the structure of a
nomad society where the women draw water and eat apart from the men, and
where girls get the habits of motherhood early. In her religious photographs too
she notices or registers a similar kind of distinction between an executive caste of
men and a shrouded mass of women. Insights also come her way, in the shape of 57
two women imprisoned by music read off the wall above their heads. Compared to
Tarnovetskij's nuanced encounters, this domestic predicament is spelt out, a
heavy moment.

But Kuznetsova's art functions in terms of differences, and this holds good of
individual pictures as well as of the ensemble. Her nomad women are, for
example, noticeably encumbered by children, burdens which stand out the more
for being seen against a background of elegant tents and waggons. Out of doors a
rough old patriarch leans like a crookedly remade river god against a crate. He
wears a quilted jacket, but his main function is to introduce a counter movement to

Lyalya Kuznetsova, Steppe, 1980

Lyalya Kuznetsova, from the cycle 'Celebrations', 1983

that of the tilted awning supported by a crooked stick. Elsewhere a loosely cloaked, dashing hero on a pedestal stands in marked contrast to a heavily encased and anything but free conductor of a military band.

Such extremes attract Kuznetsova and account for her ability to register quite different subjects. On the face of it Orthodox services and nomad life may have very little in common except that both lie well away from the secular heart of a modern society. Nor do graveyards and circus life have much thematic common ground. She is, it is true, interested in roles played by women in closed or tradition-conscious societies, yet that interest itself is no more than a function of an underlying preoccupation with freedom and constraint, the freedom of wide horizons and the nomadic life of circus people on the one hand and the claustrophobic community of the church on the other. Children enter her work as important players in the same drama, for they begin as encumbrances, they flourish and gradually fall under the sway of habit and law. One of her children, apparently releasing a captive bird, might have found a place in the great American 'Family of Man' exhibition of the 1950s, yet what is represented here is no more than an idea of freedom, for it is the bird which is at liberty rather than the child, who belongs to a society where even his juniors have learned to salute. This passage from youth to conformity was one of the main themes of the American photographer Walker Evans in the 1930s. His children eye the world at random, but the older they get the more they square up to the task in hand. Freedom, the subject implies, is no more than relative where the norms are social and cultural.

Although Kuznetsova finds plenty of evidence of the ideal, of purity and of vivacity, it never amounts to more than evidence of what might be or might have been. In one of the most impressive pictures in this or any other collection, a child marvels at an acrobat (perhaps her mother) gracefully twisted into the most unlikely shape imaginable. For that child the spectacle appears to be absolute, complete, but characteristically Kuznetsova includes bystanders for whom the only miracle is the child's amazement. The circus suits her for it signifies illusion, glamour and a time apart from the commonplace. Its performers are understood to be perpetually young or droll or courageous. Kuznetsova concentrates on the glamorous end of the market, on youth and glitter, and finds it to be down at heel, morose and wrinkled. She might have gone further backstage or joined the audience and given a more jovial account of life on stage and behind the scenes; instead she prefers to admit that her parade's gone by, that time has passed and that disintegration has set in. Nor has time dealt kindly with that young/old lady in a 55 shawl and with the manners of a girl.

There are echoes of Kuznetsova's art elsewhere in photography: just as she evokes Walker Evans's reflections on the socialization of children, so some of her portraits bring Diane Arbus's cast of characters to mind. Indeed, she has said that 'when I saw a book of photographs by Diane Arbus, I knew she had the same aim and problem'. Kuznetsova's circus women have distant relatives among Arbus's performers, and Arbus too was interested in the inadequacies of the flesh and in failures of taste. Arbus's force lay in the simplicity of her claims and contradictions, in the sheer brute force of many of her women or the obvious childishness of her males. At base she worked with regard to a set of social ideals: the film star, the soldier, the patriot. Kuznetsova, by contrast, transcends society and appears to have intuitions of other truths: those active children on the steppe, blown about by the wind, suggest more than a touch of freedom; those labyrinthine graveyards give rise to real despair, and those nomad feasts make a fine figure of plenitude. Moreover she is an observer sensitive to more than her own time and tastes: notice

Lyalya Kuznetsova, from the cycle 'Circus', 1984

that lectern-priest with his finger in the page for later reference – there are other lives out there, and other arrangements to be made.

Despite those signs of failure and decay, Kuznetsova's art is consistently beautiful. Her circus performers, even though they may feel their years, remain graceful. The nomads, after allowances for one or two dramatic ruffians, hold themselves with great dignity. Nor, despite being seen through, are her poseuses belittled and shown as mere dupes and victims of modishness. Her subjects shine, just as their precursors shone in Soviet photography during the 1920s, and this shared quality suggests one way in which her art might be understood. Although Soviet pioneer photography is usually honoured for its dynamism and modernity, many of its distinguished worker-portraits look more foursquare than dynamic; they look, in fact, not unlike icons, and certainly function as icons. The pioneers who achieved the exultant folk portraiture of the 1920s may have been moved by revolutionary enthusiasm, but at the same time they drew on Orthodox veneration for the image. In Orthodox theology, icons are not mere pictures imitative of an idea of heaven; they are of the actual stuff of redeemed creation and serve as pledges of what will be when harmony returns to the world. Nor does Orthodox theology undervalue the human image, for it expresses a likeness between Man and God and an inherent capacity on the part of humanity to become like God. In Orthodox terms the best icon or image of God is Man, and this is acknowledged in Orthodox services when the priest censes congregation as well as icons, thus saluting the image of God in that of his subjects. Kuznetsova signals this divine quality in humankind in the form of a series of gypsy madonnas who look like icons incarnate. Elsewhere in this collection Eduard Gladkov, in his studies from a Russian village, points to other continuities when he shows ancestor photographs hanging in the places once occupied by icons.

69

Kuznetsova's photographs of Orthodox worship appear at first sight to be fragmentary, to give nothing more than a flavour of traditional religion. Two are of scenes at the end of the Liturgy when the people approach to kiss a Cross held by a priest and to receive a small piece of bread called the Antidoron, blessed but not consecrated although taken from the same leavened loaf used in the consecration. In two pictures a priest and an elderly worshipper hold images of the Risen Christ. The artist thus indicates the Eucharist and the Resurrection, and in doing so indicates themes which are important in her art and in Russian art in general.

33,34

31,32

Orthodoxy lays more stress on the Incarnation than is usual in the western church; it values body and soul together and equally. Kuznetsova signals something of this enhanced regard for the material world when she shows the processional carrying of the communion bread as both a substantial and a symbolic act. In a culture where the doctrine of Transubstantiation is so vividly expressed by a church which also believes in the final redemption of all created matter, it can only be expected that the senses and appetites should be honoured by artists.

The divine glory of Christ, as manifest in the Resurrection and in the Transfiguration, is also emphasized in Orthodox worship. Transfigured on Mount Thabor He was surrounded by an Uncreated Light, a light which continued to shine in Orthodox mysticism, and which Kuznetsova expresses in the obliterating glare of reflected light on glazed images. Where the western church broods over Christ the victim, Orthodoxy exults in the Resurrection even through the humiliations of Good Friday. This theme was given a secular inflection in the photographic art of the 1920s where Man in Glory came to play the leading role. Soviet workers of that period shine with a more than natural light and enthusiasm, and it is this muted but persistent light which transforms so many of Kuznetsova's subjects.

Kuznetsova works with regard to a totality; her art is haunted by images of revolutionary destiny, Orthodox Apocalypse and the merest dreaming. Aleksandras Matsiyauskas also invokes an idea of totality when he shows his Lithuanian market as an entity, a closed world or stage bounded by a round horizon. For Kuznetsova the picture is completed elsewhere, its meaning established in relation to the Resurrection, the Incarnation or to some perfected illusion established in the circus or in the world of fashion. Matsiyauskas, in these market photographs, excludes that larger domain in favour of a circumscribed here-and-now theatrically rendered.

Photography has nothing to offer as a parallel to this art which does such violence to such an impeccable documentary subject. Country folk in both the Soviet Union and the United States constitute the nation or the backbone of the nation and are not to be represented capriciously. In Britain, on the other hand, the countryside is traditionally inhabited by 'country types' developed by novelists and caricaturists. Matsiyauskas's marketeers also look as though they might have originated in stories or in myths, for they are strongly encugh drawn to serve in any Grimm tale. In one of his most sinister images five women wait to negotiate at a produce stall; in 108 everyday terms they may be nothing more than saleswomen but photographed thus they look more like a praesidium established by the Fates to look into who knows what weakness of the flesh. In their biographical note on the artist, Daniela Mrázková and Vladimír Remeš refer to Matsiyauskas's art as metaphorical, which it certainly is; the market is his vehicle, but what is his tenor, what do the pictures portend?

The lady adjudicators appear to sit under a canopy and to form part of a circle for they are backed by other figures looking into the picture. The sellers of pigs-in-pokes (*title-page*) also appear to constitute part of a circle, kraal or laager from which they look out for clients. Sitting on top of the world they are also embattled and trapped, and these suggestions of containment are everywhere in this body of work, from the sheep who are led and bound in pairs to the travellers in waggons held in by the slatted sides. The material world, celebrated elsewhere in terms of appetite, is a heavy burden which imposes distorting pressures on its victims and acolytes. In a notable picture which might have interested Brueghel, a peasant man 110 seems about to be pushed into the ground by a sack of several overweening hundredweights of farm produce. Everywhere material seems to have been contained and to be ready to burst out of its skin, and this appearance is accentuated by the photographer's use of a wide-angle lens which represents the world as a bulging sack ready to spill its contents. A similar sort of metaphorical impulse seems to be present in Kuznetsova's pictures of intricately railed

14

graveyards, but there entrapment is certain and lamentable; Matsiyauskas, by contrast, re-enacts a struggle between an omnipresent, callous materiality and a devious mankind, up to a trick or two. His protagonists are, at the very least, prudent even sly, and might be mistaken for hunters or poachers: an introverted salesman, for instance, shows ten eggs on a net which makes it seem that they might 112 have been taken in the wild after some trouble. And that seller of toys might also be 113 a metaphor man selling versions of himself out of a secure leather bag, but choosing to keep quiet about it if those pursed lips are anything to go by.

Matsiyauskas dramatizes Man's involvement with a burdensome Nature, but does so from a child's point of view. In most photography a decent distance is kept so that there need be no sense of entanglement with the image. In this series, by contrast, material looms and no discreet distance is kept. That meeting between a cat and a goose takes place at ground level among the incidentals of the market; it is 116 the sort of detail which might be seen and noticed by that child who squints 119 playfully at the buttons on his father's coat. The seller of mannikins might also have a child in mind, and the two pigs with their owners are unnaturally imposing, more 114,115 than bristly interludes. A market is a centre for exchanges, transactions, measurement, gauging, appraisal, a conversion point where abstract, financial rules are applied to raw material. What Matsiyauskas does is to overturn those values of the market and to restore to things an original density or peculiarity; they impose themselves as they once did before habits of instrumental rationality took charge of consciousness. If this is Matsiyauskas's project it aligns him with the great American photographer Paul Strand, who often worked in close-up and from a child's eye point of view. In Strand's work, though, calculation is written into his imagery in the form of flagstones, shingled walls and other architectural details which invite enumeration. Strand's audience will be forever fallen, forever obliged to think of itself as calculating a way through material; Matsiyauskas, bringing his audience face to face with the market's plenitude, proposes a more innocent encounter with things as they gigantically are, although an idea of the market as system is always there, measured out in a clutch of eggs or a cartload of empty baskets.

Matsiyauskas is a utopian who wants to show material in its original magnificence. In so far as he is a utopian he is at one with such other Lithuanian photographers as Romualdas Rakauskas and Egons Spuris, both of whom are capable of representing their homeland as a paradise on earth. Rakauskas's blossom pictures express an idea of assimilation into a benign Nature organized along steady post-impressionist lines. In Spuris's image of children playing under a stormy sky the relationship between Man and Nature is as close, although more 86 temperamental. Lithuania in their eyes, and in those of Algimantas Kunchius, appears both as a homeland and as an ambience rather than as a site. It looks like the only properly sympathetic environment in this collection, the only landscape to arouse feeling or to answer to the moods of its devotees. In the principal non-Lithuanian landscape here, by Eduard Gladkov (*overleaf*), a horse-drawn cart leaves for an indifferent horizon. Elsewhere the land is presented – in the manner of the 1920s – as raw material waiting to be worked.

Vladimir Siomin is the only photographer here to celebrate development and the opening out of the country. Rails run, pipelines are laid and bridges built, but by wilful roustabouts rather than by the shining pioneers of the 1920s. His subject is ordinary life considered in practical, unglamorous terms. At one level his pictures, like those of Tarnovetskij, simply register small events: by a barn door at nowhere in particular an amateur barber makes enquiries and a client towels 82 loose hair from around his ears. Siomin's are representative men, although not shining examples; they get by in unpromising circumstances, just like their contemporaries anywhere else in the industrial world. But Siomin is more than just a recorder of commonplace incidents; he also develops a form or pictorial mode which embodies practical attitudes. Two of his pictures, of scattered figures idling at a weekend, appear to be in a markedly informal idiom. In one of these images four parked cars stand by a cliff top, and various strollers mark out space from the 80 middle ground into the distance. He depicts a peopled space, measurable not by virtue of anything as impalpable as atmospheric recession but in terms of human and mechanical modules. He suggests an artisan style in keeping with his handymen subjects.

Siomin with his practical interest in everyday life is a keynote photographer in this collection. He invokes Soviet idioms from the heroic decades, but where that early photography was prescriptive he is appraisive, happy to register time off. At the outset the Soviet Union only had a future; by the 1970s it had developed a considerable past and a collective memory to set with that powerful idea of a future. When Mikhajlov and Sutkus take those reflective faces in uniform they refer to a generation which has survived the future to arrive in this present where nothing grandiose seems to be in store. What is in store is everything else, including the freedom to invent like Matsiyauskas and to observe like Tarnovetskij.

By comparison with the work in this collection, contemporary western photography is by turns more assertive, more mysterious and more analytical. Much of what is publicly shown has to vie for attention in a strident art culture where Tarnovetskij's reflections on discretion would sink without trace. The pace of change in western photography also seems to be much greater; styles flourish for a term only. A photographer with Kuznetsova's range of reference and complexity of project hardly seems possible in the west, where documentary photography has, since the 1960s, been more preoccupied with style than with meaning, and more a matter of specialities (often brilliantly pursued) than of the culture at large. Kuznetsova is a major artist, not only in respect of a talent for making pictures but in the larger sense of making connections. Matsiyauskas too is one of photography's major representatives. Together the collection points to no school of Soviet photography, rather to an appraisive and more or less discreet art of the everyday.

1

1–4 Elena Darikovich

3

4

5

5–14 **Boris Savelev**

9

14

15

19

21

22

23

24

27

33

34

41

42

44

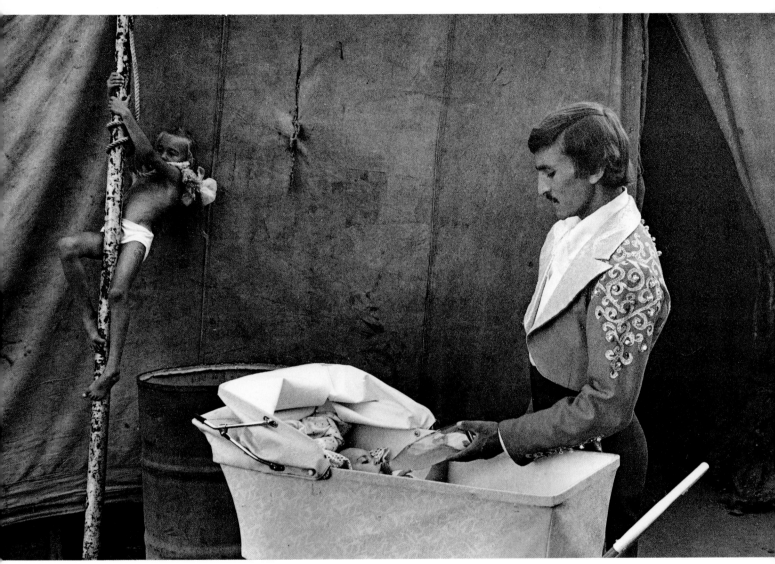

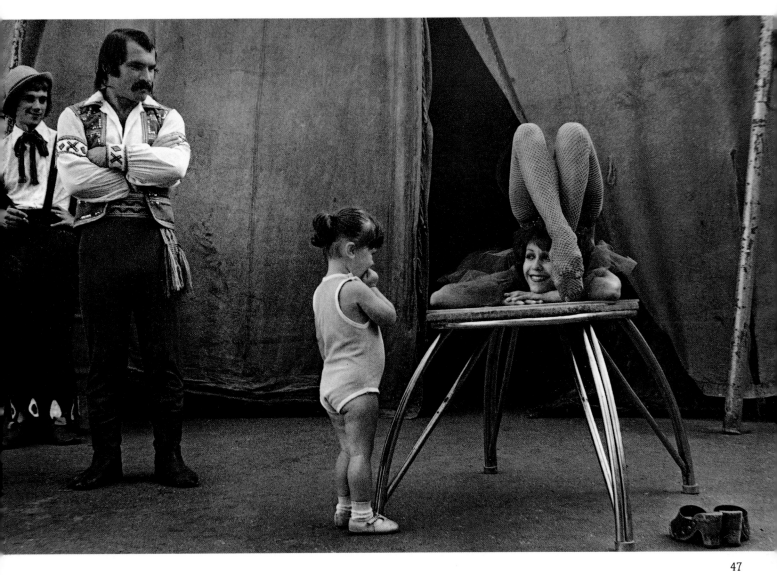

51

54

58–65 **Boris Mikhajlov**

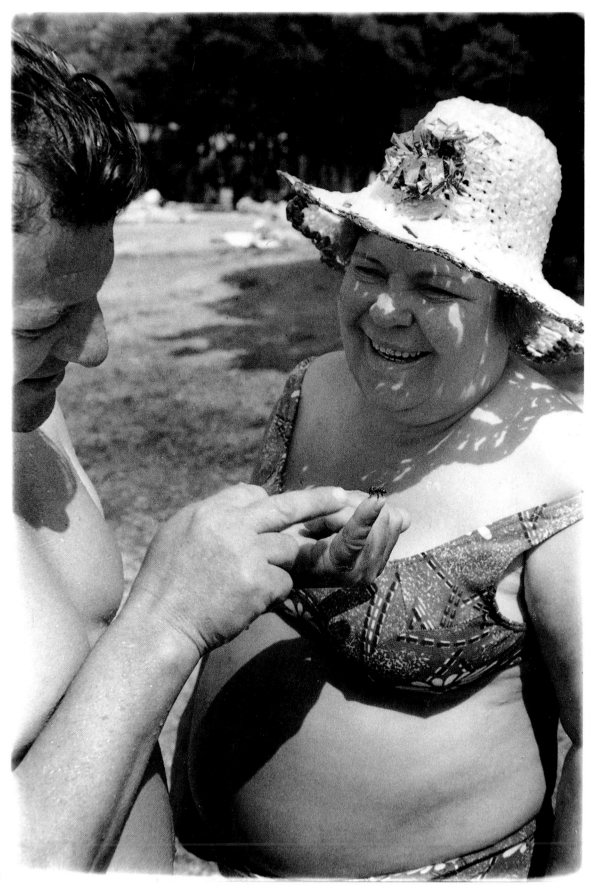

59

65

66

72

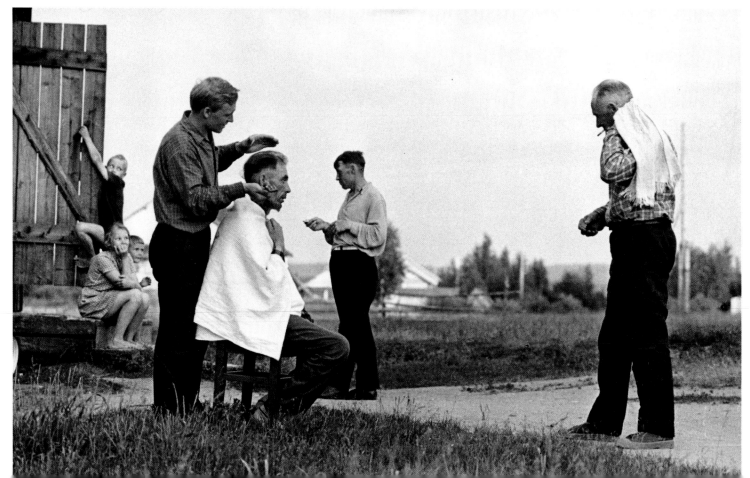

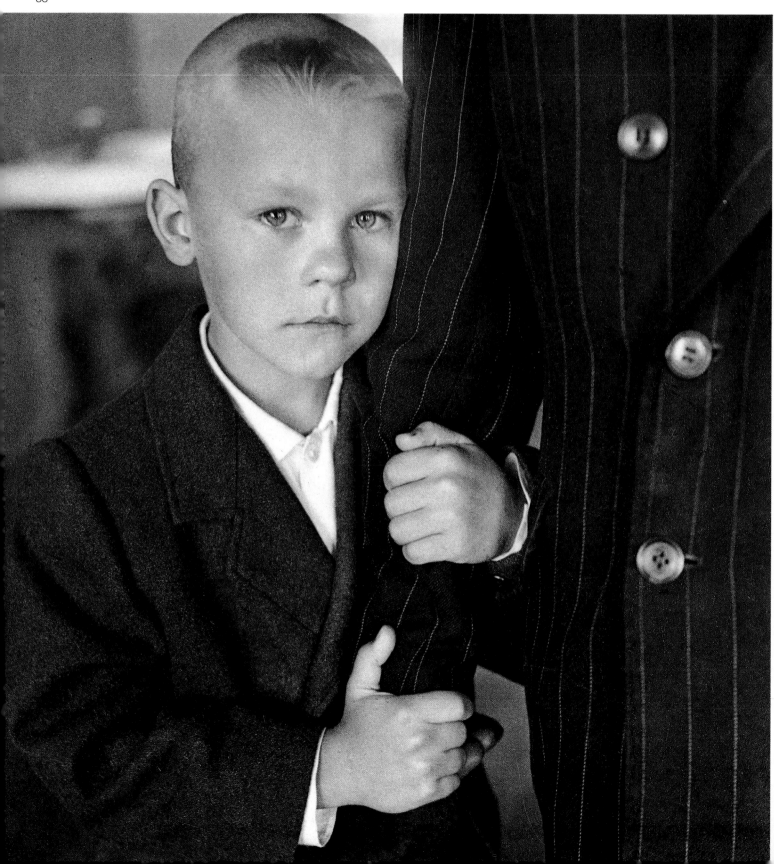

94

96

98

102–105 **Algimantas Kunchius**

106

108

111

115

116

118

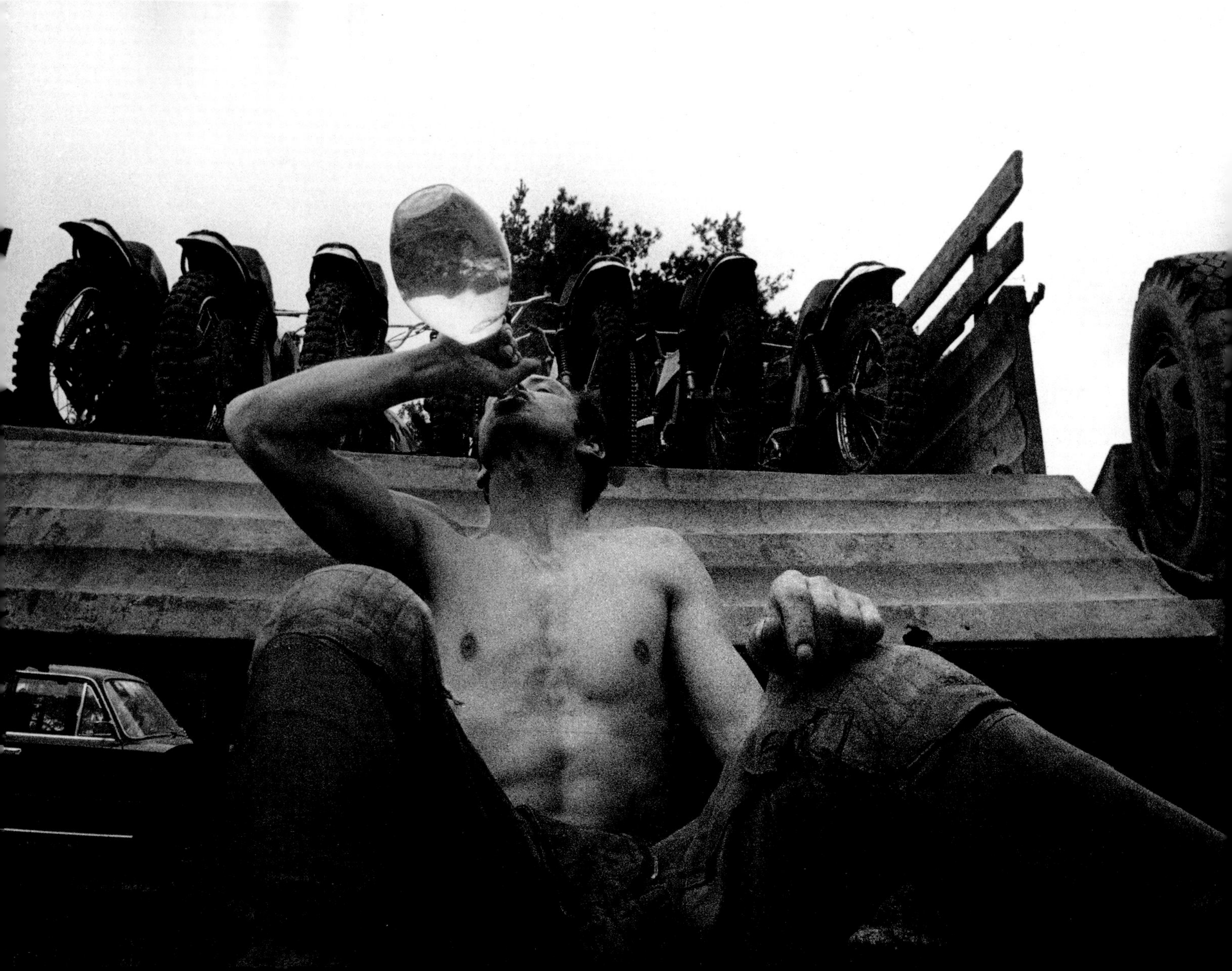

126–131 **Anatolij Garanin**

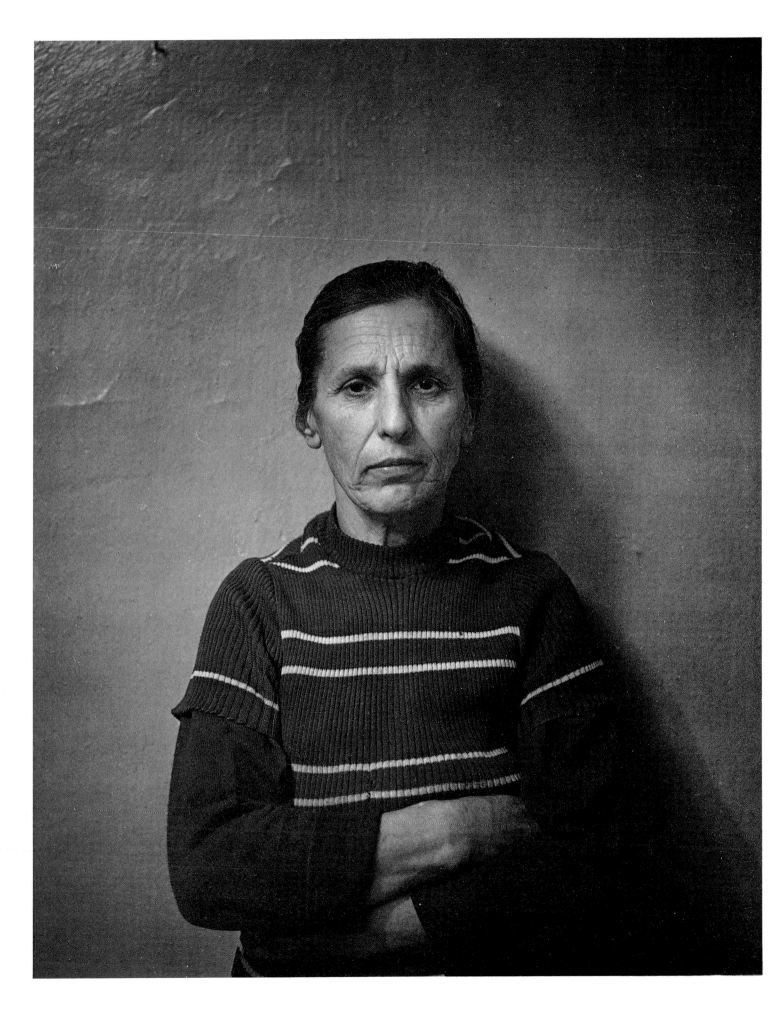

132–135 **Sergej Lopatyuk**

136

140

142

Biographies · List of plates

Elena Darikovich (b. 1951) became a photographer by chance when, after leaving school, she started to work in the photo-lab of the Museum of the Revolution in Moscow. She began taking photographs in 1976 and soon afterwards met Boris Savelev, who has had a great influence on her work. Her creative interests turned to the artificial world formed by the industrial culture in which, as a native of Moscow, she had spent her life. Like Savelev, she does not reject it, but yet cannot completely accept it either – at least not in the total form in which she encounters it every day. Her traditionally Russian sensitivity and meditativeness refuse to comply with it. 'Just as a person uprooted from his environment stops being himself, objects rid of their relationships also lose their identity and no longer evoke any emotional response. It is this emotional response that I consider to be most important in my photographic work,' explains Elena Darikovich. She takes photographs of the compact bulk of cool concrete, from behind which protrude monstrous box-like pre-fab houses, built of concrete, all looking alike, giving out a false promise of a cosy home; of human faces seemingly imprisoned by a reinforced concrete skeleton, which, however, suggests determination; of the reflection in the window pane of a contemporary Moscow tower-block that seems like a nostalgic memory of the past. Unrealistic realism is probably the most typical feature of her photographs, which wage a continuous dialogue between reality and the emotions it gives rise to.

'I photograph the signs of our time in order to come to terms with the time.' She achieves this with such vehemence that she even surpasses her teacher, Savelev. They live together in a suburb of Moscow, far from the centre, in one of the city's satellite pre-fab housing estates. Their house is pre-fab, with pre-fab facilities; only the living room is evidence of rebellion against the uniformity of modern life: it is left entirely empty, to provide a space for desires, ideas and dreams. It is an island, an open space, an oasis, but also a challenge to the bourgeois narrow-mindedness of our time.

Elena travels twenty-five kilometres every day to reach the publishing house where she works as a photographer. Only at weekends can she work on her own photographs, but she is always able to find time for discussions with her friends – photographers, artists, writers, all in their thirties – even at midnight or six in the morning.

1 **Boris, 1984**
2 **Moscow, 1984**
3 **Underground bridge, 1984**
4 **Caricyno, 1984**

Boris Savelev (b. 1948) belittles his photographs by calling them *photocartochki* ('photo-cards'), thus implying that he has nothing in common with the academic conception of a photograph. 'My impressions of life are expressed by snapshots of towns – Moscow and Leningrad – and as I believe that one can get the best idea of the life of a person from his environment and from the objects that surround him, I therefore photograph this environment and these objects.'

He takes his snapshots continuously, finding his subject wherever he goes – on the pavement, on the underground train, on a bridge, in a park, on a wall, in the corner of an arcade or yard. He piles them up in the small house in a Moscow suburb which he shares with the photographer Elena Darikovich and prefers to show them instead of talking. 'I have nothing special to say, but here are my shots. It's not art, they are only *photocartochki*, I've got hundreds of them.'

Savelev's work is a continuous chain of impressions, reflections and contemplations, created as a basic, vital human urge. He considers it of paramount importance 'to include in a picture all its individual components in relationships which correspond to personal feelings', but this does not mean that he waits for hours for the right moment when everything in front of his lens is in an ideal position: his vision is spontaneous. His *photocartochki*, seemingly taken purely by chance, are actually the result of a sharp reaction to reality, perceived in arrangements which reflect his feelings. He creates spacious picture mosaics which are true documents of the inner world of a man of a specific generation, time and place.

Savelev, who is a graduate of the Institute of Aeronautics, has taken photographs since childhood, but he started to work systematically only in 1970, when he became a member of the popular Moscow photo-club Novator. From the very beginning he was interested in people's way of life and was greatly impressed by the photographs of Eugène Atget and Walker Evans. Step by step he abandoned the depiction of reality from the outside and began to view it through the prism of his feelings – the feelings of a person confined by the anxieties and desires engendered by the limits of the contemporary world of a developed civilization. His pictures became void of action and gradually also of people as their main subjects. He started to put special stress on free open spaces, on minute, almost trite, details, on outlines, tonality and the mystery of vistas and reflections.

The more he subsided into himself, the less was he interested in his technical career, which he finally abandoned in 1982; he is now a freelance photographer working for various Soviet publishing houses. Savelev has become the binding force for a group of the new generation of photographers which has turned away from the main current of a straightforwardly expressive art; they conceive of photography as a testimony of the most profound states of the human soul, as an investigative 'search for the truth about the human condition here and now'.

5   Moscow, 1980
6   Leningrad, 1984
7   Moscow, 1982
8   Moscow, 1982
9   Leningrad, 1983
10 In the bus, 1983
11 Moscow, 1982
12 Moscow, 1982
13 Leningrad, 1984
14 Moscow, 1982

Aleksandr Slyusarev (b. 1944) was made known to the general public by his friend the Latvian photographer Egons Spuris, who is also included in this book. After some years of quiet work, unknown to almost anybody, Slyusarev came to attention as late as 1979 when he exhibited his work as a guest at the annual photographic festival of the Baltic republics in the small town of Ogre, near Riga, the capital of the Latvian SSR. He presented a large collection of intimate pictures of his home environment which were very well received. 'They labelled me as a photographer of the external world, but that is quite wrong. I take photos of everything: objects are of interest to me only with regard to the relationship that is established between them and me. Only then do the connections of the object with planes, points and lines – with the other components of the future picture – gain their importance.'

Slyusarev started to take photographs very early, at the age of fifteen. From the beginning he was influenced by the Czechoslovak photographic quarterly *Revue fotografie* and so as early as the late 1950s was acquainted with a type of photography different from the schematically conceived, lifeless photojournalism which he encountered at exhibitions and in books and magazines. In the *Revue* he discovered the work of photographers from various countries, including the Soviet Union, at a time when most Soviet photographers were unable to publish anywhere else because their photographs were unlike those officially recognized. He thus came to understand that the language of photography need not be pretentious and noisily celebratory but can also be very intimate. This former designer understands the importance of the aesthetic aspect, but does not allow it dominance; he knows that it must also go hand in hand with the statement which is being conveyed. His highly sophisticated pictures attract many young creative artists – painters and graphic designers as well as photographers – who come to visit him in his Moscow home from all over the country. He himself takes

photographs only in his spare time; for years he has made his living by translating from Italian.

'For the last three years I have been photographing very little, usually for series devoted to a specific subject. In this way I created Chologov 82 – dealing with my personal response to the life of a town near Moscow – Leningrad 83 and Riga 84. In the final selection these series consist of one hundred to one hundred and fifty photographs – in exceptional instances as many as two hundred. And even though every picture is a part of a larger whole, I try to take them in such a way for them to be so strong both visually and in terms of their meaning that they can exist independently – by themselves.'

15 Šaulaj, 1981
16 Moscow, 1983
17 Leningrad, 1983
18 Pavement, 1981

Lyalya Kuznetsova (b. 1946) comes from west Kazachstan in the Urals and is of Tartar blood. She studied at the Institute of Aeronautics, specialized in aeroplane engines, married an aeronautic engineer and for some time worked with him. Then in 1976 she was widowed. As a help to recovery she decided to look around for something completely new to do, and quite by chance she started to take photographs. At once her exceptional talent made itself visible; it was as though she had learnt a language more expressive and telling than the one she had been using since her cradle.

In 1980, Antanas Sutkus, the president of the Society for Creative Photography of the Lithuanian SSR, saw her work and invited her to Vilnius. For eighteen months she worked there as an employee of the Society and soon gained recognition at exhibitions. She decided to leave the job, although it had been the means by which she had attracted attention, partly because she could not speak Lithuanian but largely because she felt suffocated by the academic and conventional atmosphere of Lithuanian photography, which had been the dominant influence in Soviet photography since the 1960s. 'All those public appearances, the need to exhibit oneself and the desire to show-off – all that is not my problem,' Kuznetsova has said. 'I do not want to seize possession of reality, but only quietly approach it. I want to make documents of the human soul.'

She returned to the Volga steppe. Having photographed for a children's magazine and for a children's theatre in Kazan', she has since 1983 been working as a freelance. But she really only comes alive with subjects of her own choosing. She is attracted mainly by unconventional people – nomads, circus performers – or people in exceptional circumstances – funerals, holidays and festivities. 'I am attracted by the free lives of the nomads,' she has said. 'For weeks I wander through the steppe with them and live their kind of life. Usually they are expecting me, because news of me flies from one camp to another, but sometimes a camp does not trust me and rejects me. Once a woman gave me a real beating out of jealousy, but I was not angry. I understood her feelings.' Kuznetsova's view of the nomads' life was at first romantic, but the more she came to understand them the more did her vision of the legendary heroes of the steppe in the midst of unbounded nature recede, together with the taint of Russian realist painting, and her photographs started to reflect the hard reality of people without a home, constantly driven by a sense of unrest. The same can be said about her pictures of circus performers – the tight-rope walkers, jugglers, wild-animal tamers and magicians; she photographs them not under the spotlight but in the moments before they put on their glittering costumes and the insouciant masks of courageous professionals.

Kuznetsova works a great deal, easily and rapidly. The exceptional creative passion, even insatiability, with which she has amassed new subjects has, during the few years in which she has been seriously taking photographs, shaped an artistic personality which has such an intuitive feel for subjects and the passing moment that we can infer almost everything about the psychic and social situation of the world in which she lives. In this she is a real master. In her picture series on the traditional Orthodox religion, the May Day celebrations, the last things of man, the rallies for the anniversary of the socialist revolution or on such simple things as a woman's soul, Kuznetsova's photographs tell stories like those of only the greatest writers.

Boris Mikhajlov (b. 1938) comes from Khar'kov, the industrial centre of north-east Ukraine, where he works as a professional photographer. Originally he worked in adult education and thus is well informed about people's sparetime activities. He has a very precise programme: to find out what people do when they are not working and whether their leisure pursuits bring them pleasure and contentment.

He has said about his work that 'I believe in the force of a series of photographs on one subject: it has a greater impact than individual pictures. I therefore deal with my subjects in cycles. My creative creed? To be always catching the constant changes, because in front of my eyes everything that should be photographed is disappearing rapidly. What I am interested in today has by tomorrow already become the past and it is up to us, the photographers, to catch the rapid transformations of our life.'

He has produced cycles entitled 'Dance', 'Beach', 'Park' and 'Women's Gymnastics' which deal with the activities of the great mass of people. The photographs show festivities in which women dance with each other, recalling the times when the men had gone to the war and women had to take their roles. And the war veterans, those who were lucky enough to survive? They stand apart, wearing their old army caps – every part of a military uniform is held in high esteem here – and a medal on their Sunday coat or Russian shirt. They watch the dancing condescendingly, for life never gave them time to learn to dance.

The cycle 'Beach' is devoted to the pleasure-seeking of people relaxing in the spas of the Sea of Azor and to Festivals of the Folk which take place in the Parks of Leisure even in winter, when people play ball, skittles and other games. He treats women's gymnastics with his characteristic kindly amusement. The enthusiastic competing of young women who could be anything but real gymnasts fascinates because of the atmosphere of pleasure derived from movement and a feeling of feminine self-assertion. In his professional capacity Mikhajlov also takes many colour pictures, but his more austere black-and-white photographs are better suited to his documentary programme and they are the means to sensitive social analysis. These are the annals of everyday life. Mikhajlov does not judge; he is a clever observer of his environment, an indulgent glosser of humanity.

Eduard Gladkov (b. 1939) has for many years been working on a project with the courageous title 'Moscow and all its people'. 'It is the result of all my previous efforts and searching,' he explained in his defence. 'Theoretical and practical. A social analysis of a metropolis. Before I realized what I really wanted to do, I took portrait photos of various personalities in culture, science and art and worked for several editors. But I actually discovered myself only in this documenting of Moscow life. I started to understand the spirit of my town and the feelings one has when one lives in it. I realized that a photograph is essentially a document.'

Gladkov is a native of Moscow. He grew up there, studied oceanography at the Moscow State University and now lives and works in the city as a photojournalist. He left his original profession to become a photographer three years after graduating and for three years he worked as a photojournalist for the magazine *Krylia rodiny* (*Wings of the Country*). In 1974 he began to teach photography at the Peoples' University of Art. Having worked for some time as a freelance photographer, in 1983 he joined the magazine *Studencheski Meridian* (*Students' Meridian*). 'In the course of my life I've devoted more time to earning a living than to photography,' he laconically summarized the years of search for his own project. 'I started to take photographs for a purpose only in 1980.'

Another undertaking is a still-to-be completed documentary cycle 'The village of Tchachnicy and all its people'. Unlike his Moscow project, this scheme does not exceed the boundaries of what one man can do in a lifetime. Tchachnicy is a smallish village in which Gladkov started to take photographs in 1982. It is hard to believe that it is only a few miles from Moscow and all its commotion. It lives at a slow pace, its life marked out by sunset and sunrise and the four seasons. Perhaps only its bedridden members note, from the pages of newspapers and from the small portable TV set, how close the great industrial and social centre is and what an impact it has had on civilization.

Gladkov creates documentaries which notice everything down to the smallest detail: beds made the old-fashioned way, the heavy straddling posture of a hard-working man, revered family pictures hung on the wall where the icons used to be. From this detailed description he builds up his understanding of the quality of a life that is hard, unadorned, perhaps happy, certainly honest. 'My aim is the free reflection of the varied reality with which I am surrounded, a life evolving in sharp contrasts.'

66–71   From the cycle 'The village of Tchachnicy and all its people', 1982

Vladimir Siomin (b. 1938) has written 'My fate as a photographer depends on the people I meet. They are the embodiment of the time and the place in which I live. It is my great ambition to depict objectively the atmosphere of our life, and therefore I carefully select my encounters with people.' It has not always been easy for Siomin to achieve his aim. His sober, externally undynamic, often static pictures were received with mixed feelings by the editors of the newspapers and picture agencies he worked for.

At the end of the 1970s Siomin stayed in Siberia for several months to observe the construction of the Baikul-Amur Track railway (BAM). He did not bring back to Moscow the usual pictures of the efforts of a new, young generation or of impressive heroes, but a sociological study of the existence of those who for various reasons decided to abandon their way of life and move to the pioneer conditions at the far end of the country. He lived with them in caravans, old railway carriages and huts, up to

his knees in mud or snow. He composed his photographic record from small details of everyday life: time for a cigarette before the empty truck returns and will have to be reloaded; a moment of rest next to the newly laid tracks in the early evening; a tired foreman gesticulating that the truck can move on; men competing in a pub in the evening; skipping children growing up on a building site; a flirtation with a girl at the canteen counter. The basic things of life, here as anywhere, but shaped differently by the rough conditions of Siberia. It recalls the lives of conquerors of unknown lands, where ordinary things become special because they have to be paid for by exceptional effort and sacrifices, and where man again feels the need to live in symbiosis with nature.

Siomin's pictures clearly stand apart from the emotive celebratory mode of traditional photojournalism, whether he is photographing BAM and its legends of heroism, or other far-off places – Dagestan, Baskiria and Karelia. On his expeditions he looks for people, not for pictures to illustrate a thesis. 'I systematically set out on the path of the commonplace, which in my opinion is the only way to portray the truth about life' he explained. Today he is respected largely by the younger generation of photographers, who also avoid traditional symbolism, pathos and romanticism, turning instead to a vision that is sober and matter-of-fact.

Vladimir Siomin was born in Yasna Poliana, which lies amid the fields and forests of Russia's central plain. He graduated from a school of mechanical engineering and immediately began work as a technician in Murmansk, in the north. When only ten years old he had started to take photographs under the guidance of his elder brother and since then he has considered photography to be a basic part of his life, although it was only during his military service that he decided to become a photographer. He left his profession and at the age of twenty-two started to work as a freelance photographer, later becoming a film-news photographer in Rostov-na-Donu and then a photojournalist in Tula. To extend his education he went to study at the faculty of literature of Petrozavodsk University, from which he graduated in 1967. Since then he has worked for factory newspapers and, in the 1970s, as a photojournalist for the picture agency APN in Moscow, for whom he travelled over all the USSR. He is now a freelance photographer.

72–78   From the cycle 'Construction of the Baikul-Amur Track, Siberia', 1978–80
79   Festival of spring, Kubatchi village, Dagestan, 1982
80   Rochata village, Caucausas, 1983
81   Holiday in the Nogayskiye steppe, 1982
82   Muasalmi village, Karelia, 1984
83   Easter day in Baskiria, 1983

Rifkhat Yakupov (b. 1944) grew up amid the organized amateur photography movement, which in the USSR is subsidized by the government and the trade unions. Born in Izhevsk, he is a Tartar by nationality. He graduated from the faculty of journalism at Kazan' University in 1969, but two years later he turned to photography and gave up writing. Making good use of the experience he had gained in amateur photography, he became a photojournalist on the staff of the Tartar magazine for women *Azat-ćhatyn* (*Liberated Woman*). In 1974 he became a member of the photography group TAMSA in Kazan', which includes both amateurs and professionals, and participates in its richly varied programme of exhibitions.

His magazine job involves photographing almost everything, from political news to agricultural, industrial and social events, but his most frequent subject – both at work and in his own photography – is life in the Tartar villages. He photographs the tiny houses set along the slopes of the steppe, the arid dusty soil, the endless deserted landscapes seemingly created for horses to roam. Here are villagers in the peaceful atmosphere of a Sunday afternoon who appear not to know what to do with their normally busy hands, Tartar women in their traditional clothes and everywhere masses of energetic children. The aesthetic approach to documentary, characteristic of Yakupov's work, suggests the strong influence of the Lithuanian photographers – an influence which he is proud to admit. But Lithuanian romanticism is not a feature of his photographs, probably because life on the steppe is so much harsher than on the Baltic shores.

84–85 Tartar village, 1984

Egons Spuris (b. 1931) is regarded as the most typical of the Lithuanian photographers, whose work, like that of photographers in the other Soviet Baltic republics, has advanced greatly since the 1960s. He photographs the rugged, melancholy country of the Baltic coast; his nostalgically spacious, barren landscapes are usually shot with a wide-angle lens, as is the fashion in the Baltic countries. Heavy clouds dominate his photographs, whose dramatically expressive nature depends on his interest in the possibilities of surface and structure: sand furrowed by the wind; coarse tufts of grass lonely but defiant in the midst of the dunes; the dark line of the sea on the far horizon; the silhouette of a ship seemingly cast up by the waves; in the foreground, a dead fish, an alabaster boulder weathered by the elements – these are the realities of the region in which Spuris lives and the symbols by which he expresses his profound experiences.

However, he does not photograph only landscapes. His range extends from intimate portraits to still-lives on urban themes. Essentially a Neo-Romantic, he is not unaware of the development of photography elsewhere towards the documentary. Although not following that trend, he has taken over many of its techniques of expression. So he has created a new approach to physical reality, preserving its inner romantic charge. Objects seem to have lost their original function, to be discarded from the life they served

or were supposed to serve. Deprived of their original purpose, they are some kind of tragic memento of a loneliness which affects not only the world of people, but also the things that are indispensable to it. Spuris notices their shapes, seeming to fondle and caress them as though in silent dialogue with them, suddenly uncovering the great mysterious secret of yet undiscovered phenomena. He is also interested in architectural ensembles, the juxtaposition of historic and modern and the geometry of rooftops, streets and squares. He frequently uses these subjects to make sharp contrasts between traditional life and the products of technical progress, symbolizing the transformations of ways of life.

Spuris began as an amateur; his photos won awards at exhibitions from Riga to Toronto and Ceylon. Nobody today would take him for a blacksmith, which he became at the age of seventeen. He began to attend extramural courses and made his way from laboratory assistant to engineer to designer at the VEF factory of radios and audiovisual technology in Riga. Later he lectured at the Polytechnical Institute in Riga, where he had once studied. In 1976–8 he was chief designer of the Office of Industrial Design in Riga and later art director of the Riga People's Photo Studio, where he teaches photographers and organizes Lithuanian photographic events.

86 Latvian boys, 1980
87 Latvian landscape, 1980

Antanas Sutkus (b. 1938) has declared that 'photography is my way of communicating with people'. He takes photographs 'because in them lies the truth of our life. Because I feel responsible to the coming generations that will judge us one day. My main aim is to create a psychological portrait of the man of today.'

Sutkus was born in the Lithuanian village Kluoniskiai, on the banks of the frontier river Nemen. His childhood and youth were marked by tragedy, linked with political developments in Lithuania. His father, a labourer in a factory in Kaunas and a well-known Communist official, committed suicide as a protest against the Stalinist denial of the right of self-determination of small nations. Antanas Sutkus was then one year old. His mother remarried, but soon again lost her husband, in the turmoil of World War II, when Antanas was three. He can recall the local police, working for the occupying Germans, looking for his father, whom they believed had gone underground, and for his stepfather, but by then both were dead. At the age of sixteen he became ill with tuberculosis of the kidneys and had to spend many months in a sanatorium. It was then that he became interested in photography. Finally, his mother died, on her birthday, at the end of his convalescence. When he retells all this, it seems he has no reason to see life as it appears in his photographs.

Sutkus started to regard photography seriously only when at university in Vilnius, where he read history and philosophy. His interest in social subjects was his expression of protest against doctrinaire contemporary photography. His pictures brought new life to the fossilized Soviet photography of the 1950s. It was a fresh wave of optimistic photographs, fragments of immanent life – people in various moods, laughing, pensive, excited or caught at moments of purely private thought; old men and women, lovers, village youngsters; all the attributes of traditional life – geese, hens and scores of children – set in a melancholy low-lying countryside, seemingly without any horizon, enclosed by earth and sky. Yet they are very human photographs, full of honest simplicity and happiness derived from life. Few Soviet photographers, except for those in the Baltic regions, could then equal him.

Sutkus thus personifies the fermentation that took place in the cultural life of his region after Stalin's death and the end of the personality cult, a fermentation which finally resulted in 1969 in the creation of the state-supported Society for Creative Photography of the Lithuanian SSR. Sutkus was its spiritual father and the initiator of modern concepts of photographic education, exhibitions, unconventional creative seminars – all the characteristics of Lithuanian organized photography. From its beginnings to the present day he has always been either the president or vice-president of the Society.

'People of Lithuania' is the name of Sutkus's never ending cycle of freely linked pictures which is not bound by any subject but is constantly supplemented and developed from new points of view. It is conceived of in general terms as reportage and although Sutkus has long ago given up his socio-critical interests his main attention is still devoted to the pictorial analysis of the social structure.

88–95 From the cycle 'People of Lithuania', 1970–85

Romualdas Rakauskas (b. 1941) has provoked controversy among his colleagues. 'For some time I quarrelled with Rakauskas, because he absolutely refused to admit the part played by imagination in the photographic rendition of an idea' proclaimed Aleksandras Matsiyauskas at one of the large public meetings of Lithuanian photographers, 'and now we encounter this very phenomenon in his photographs.' The discussion – in which not only photographers, but also artists, film critics, art historians and even writers and poets participated – concerned Rakauskas's picture series 'Blossoming', which he had been working on since 1976. Rakauskas voluntarily stood 'in the dock', to be judged by his colleagues and friends; like improvised outdoor exhibitions, these open discussions are a regular part of Lithuanian photographic life.

Rakauskas, who is generally called a Neo-Romantic, introduced with this cycle new qualities into the depiction of Lithuanian life. As with all Lithuanian photography from its beginnings, he too tried to create symbols of a happy life. The people in his photographs were usually in motion and the feeling of joy was reinforced by his treatment of the landscape's texture, overexposed by the low northern sun – cold, but with an inner warmth, producing pictures which

are clear-cut down to the most microscopic details. However, since about the mid-1970s this ostentatious joy has disappeared from Rakauskas's pictures. Dynamic motion has also receded. His interest has shifted to a documentary approach which is emotionally more restrained yet has greater profundity. He seems to be attempting to reveal not only men but also their close links with their environment.

As 'Blossoming' shows, he still chooses subjects that are beautiful and pleasing, sometimes even pretty-pretty. But he has a brilliant sense of the precise limits of the superficially attractive; he creates a balanced contrast of romantic and documentary elements. The snow-white pointillist spots of the blossom and leaves construct the pictures in a purely photographic way. Against this background of a white flood of blossoms, so realistic as to look almost unreal, he deals with specific subjects – an old married couple sitting at a table, for instance, or a beehive, a hen in the yard, a boy cradling a rabbit, or a row of village children. Their arrangement and the frontal views often resemble old family photographs. It is this confrontation of the romantic motif and the documentary style that provokes by its incongruity, even grotesqueness. The result is a portrait of a modern sensibility, of a longing for dreams which yet constantly encounters reality. It represents Rakauskas's constant return to his childhood, to a time when life was contained in the close link between man and nature. He has never detached himself from the way of life of the Lithuanian village Akmeneje, where he was born, although he studied journalism at Vilnius University and since the mid-1960s has been working for the Vilnius magazine *Nemunas*, which plays an important role in the cultural life of the republic.

96–101 From the cycle 'Blossoming', 1976–85

Algimantas Kunchius (b. 1939) studied law at Vilnius University, but its austere rigour caused him to move to the Teachers' Training Institute, where he specialized in music. However, after graduation he did not become a teacher but began to work as a photographer for newspapers and journals. In 1963 he became a photojournalist for the weekly *Literatura irmajanas* (*Literature and Art*) and two years later he joined the editorial board of *Kulturos baraj* (*Milestone of Culture*). By then he was already a member of the Lithuanian photographers' movement, which was striving for national identity. Together with Antanas Sutkus, Aleksandras Matsiyauskas, Romualdas Rakauskas and other young photographers, he introduced into photography subjects from ordinary, unembellished life, marked by the traditions of Lithuanian national culture. In 1969 he became a joint founder of the Society for Creative Photography of the Lithuanian SSR and was elected the chairman of its art council.

Like most of the Lithuanian photographers, he is primarily interested in village subjects. He too comes from the country – the small town Pakruois – and is familiar with the character of rural people. He has accumulated thousands of pictures of his special subject, 'Village Sunday'. It reflects what has survived in his country of an ancient tradition and shows the close relationship between people as well as their close links with nature. On Sundays everybody dresses in their best clothes to visit each other, giving way, after the week's work, to their natural longing for conviviality. Those who live in hamlets outside the villages come to join them. On the village common or in some customary place in the open countryside, free from their everyday worries, they find time to eat, drink, gossip and dance to an accordion. In the evening even those who have a long way to go sit down on the grass, unpack their supplies and share their supper. Kunchius conveys the atmosphere of these festive occasions as well as the spacious character of the villages in the open countryside. He knows how to present the rural types – dignified countrymen in dark suits with the indispensable hat or visored caps, kind old women in kerchiefs, emancipated aunties keen to dance, youthful defiant labourers, young girls in their finery and innumerable children. His photographs reveal the admiration he feels for these ordinary people at whose precarious life he looks with understanding and wistful humour. At the beginning of the 1980s Kunchius stopped working for magazines and became a paid consultant of the Society for Creative Photography of the Lithuanian SSR, thus returning to teaching, his original profession.

102–105 From the cycle 'Village Sunday', 1975–85

Aleksandras Matsiyauskas (b. 1938) for ten years photographed nothing but village markets, even when told that he was ignoring the present and idealizing the past. He has been systematic to the point of wilfulness, even though his work as photoreporter for the Lithuanian daily *Vakarines naujieons* has frequently interfered with his intentions. Since 1979 he has also been engaged in a study called 'The veterinary clinic' but 'Village markets' is not yet complete.

Matsiyauskas has created an extensive record of the ancient tradition of the Lithuanian villagers, who from almost as far back as the Middle Ages have come together after the harvest in a large, lively market. All are both actors and spectators in a extraordinary show: horses, geese, cows, hens, piles of potatoes, home-made products; the people sell, buy, try to shout each other down, the pigs grunt, the geese cackle, and children run excitedly here and there. But this is all only the context. What the photographer is really interested in is the types of people, their typical modes of trading, their passions and relationships. Here they bargain, fight, lament, grudge, rejoice, with room for neighbourly jokes and gossip. In Matsiyauskas's hands, with the aid of unusual angles and the effect of a wide-angle lens, this popular show appears as though under a magnifying glass: a pig's head grows to unnatural size by an enlarged close-up, people seen from a low viewpoint are given an unrealistic significance, steep perspectives lend a special dynamism to their normal actions and everyday gestures.

Matsiyauskas's extensive reportage project is not an attempt to embalm the past; he shows how this ancient tradition fulfils social as well as practical needs, for it is also an entertainment. This is a sociological analysis of human types, of men shaped by their village, of the mentality of a nation which is naturally bound by its customs and by the culture of the past.

Aleksandras Matsiyauskas was born in the Lithuanian town Kaunas. After completing his secondary school education he studied at the University of Marxism-Leninism in Vilnius for two years. He is one of the founders of modern Lithuanian photography and its central organization, the Society for Creative Photography of the Lithuanian SSR, of which he is at present full-time executive secretary. As with those friends who share his opinions, it is the expressive possibilities of photography that are most characteristic of his work. As a matter of principle, he uses a wide-angle lens, which enables him to make his pictures heroic and poetic but also ironic, transmuting the documentary mode into the metaphorical, as well as forcing him to take close-ups, thus putting himself at the centre of events. It was primarily his example that opened the door for spontaneous, lively pictures in Soviet photography. His photographic creed is based on the principle which he attempts to adhere to in his life: 'Tell the truth, only the truth, and once again the truth if you want to consider yourself a humanist.'

106–121 From the cycle 'Village markets', 1972–84

Romualdas Pozherskis (b. 1951) became interested in photography in 1963, when he was twelve, and was closely linked with the very beginning of the surprising emergence of the Lithuanian photographers. After graduating as a civil engineer from the Polytechnical Institute in Vilnius, he began work in 1975 for the Kaunas branch of the Society for Creative Photography of the Lithuanian SSR and has been a professional photographer ever since. He began by making a study of certain subjects in the form of cycles of photographs, and he has maintained his interest in those subjects now that he works as a freelance photographer. One of these cycles, 'Victories and defeats', has drawn praise from his older colleagues, including Aleksandras Matsiyauskas, whom Pozherskis regards as his teacher.

Pozherskis is fascinated by dramatic sports competitions, in particular motorcar racing, for they provide an opportunity to depict not only the competitors in action but also the hidden backstage atmosphere and the drivers' feelings. He photographs them at moments of concentration just before the start, or exhausted and tired after the race. He is interested in their desires, their unfulfilled hopes, their happiness after a victory and the strain of defeat. The subject itself – tension at the race-track, machines, youths and their admiration for anything technical – has an impact very different from the traditional interest of Lithuanian photographers in the relationship of man and nature. Yet, like Matsiyauskas in his 'Village markets' cycle, Pozherskis photographs exclusively with a wide-angle lens. The expressive language of his photography stresses the uniqueness and unreality of extreme situations in human life.

122–125   From the cycle 'Victories and defeats', 1975–84

Anatolij Garanin (b. 1912) has spent his entire career as a journalist, assigned to produce photographs of important political and official events both at home and abroad, but he is far from the popular image of a press photographer. He is attracted not by external, but by internal dramas, hidden deep under the surface of the visible world. This was also true of his work in World War II, during which he was constantly in the front line taking hundreds of photographs, some today very famous, but he remembers little of this time, as he was, he says, always in a trance. War was foreign to his all-consuming desire for harmony, cultivated in him by his deep love for music; it is also the denial of his basic values of life, the humanism which he professes; it involves great drama, which he always tries to avoid.

Garanin is full of contradictions. Since the 1950s he has worked as special correspondent of the picture magazine *Soviet Union*, which publicizes the USSR abroad, and with characteristic care he has created picture essays to order. For his private work, however, he chooses his subjects carefully, like a gourmet. His great love is music and theatre. He likes music to be majestic and prefers the pre-Romantic periods. When he listens he closes his eyes, his face reflects his delight and despite his physical robustness he seems to be floating, in harmony with the music.

'At concerts I do not photograph the musicians, whom I hardly notice, but their music,' he explained. He has worked for all the Moscow theatres, and is permanent photographer for the avant-garde theatres Sovremennik, Malaia Bronnaia and Theatre Na Taganke. Whenever they produce a new play, Garanin becomes infected with enthusiasm; he neither sees nor hears but lives only for his photographs, from the first rehearsals to the opening night. The directors and actors think of him as part and parcel of the theatre. It is this very youthful passion that brings him close to the present generation of photographers, who are also interested in expressing spontaneous experience.

In various ways Garanin artificially disturbs his pictures so as to give them a particular emotional effect. He puts his fingers in front of the lens, sometimes covering most of the space, so as to make an important feature prominent. He frequently uses out of focus shots, distortions and reflections, and often makes a minute detail the central element of a picture. People in his photographs are always serious and inward looking, as if their stillness or activity were conditioned by a strong inner tension.

126   Professor Nadezhda Artobarevskaya of the Moscow Conservatory

127   Professor Tichon Krennikov with his pupils at the Moscow Conservatory

128   Galina Voltchek, chief director of the Moscow theatre Sovremennik

129   Georgi Tovstonogov, chief director of the Leningrad Bolshoi theatre

130   Leonid Brezhnev

131   Dmitri Shostakovitch

Sergej Lopatyuk (b. 1955) lives in Chernovtsy, in the most western corner of the Ukraine. He lectures on theoretical physics at the local university and at the universities of several other Ukrainian towns. He takes photographs in his spare time, but only at home, in Chernovtsy. 'I believe that photographs should not be the result of chance. They should be a way of looking at things, the result of thought. I consider it to be the photographer's individual responsibility to record only the things he knows well. For me personally a thorough study of the subject is essential, which is why I take photographs only at home.'

Photography has been a relief from his demanding scientific work. Since his student days he has followed the example of his older colleague, Vyacheslav Tarnovetskij, who is also a physicist. From him he learned the force and possibilities of photography and Lopatyuk's first exhibition, in the Lithuanian town Siauliai in 1981, was held jointly with Tarnovetskij.

Lopatyuk is mostly interested in people and their environment. His desire to be accurate and truthful is reflected in his almost stringent austerity. People usually look directly into his lens; the importance of objects for the required statement seems to be calculated well in advance. The sober composition of each picture is determined by a desire to give it a clear meaning. He is uncompromising in his insistence that each picture fill the 6 × 6 cm viewfinder of his reflex camera. He will not crop his pictures, explaining that 'we crop our lives in such a way that we cannot afford to crop photographs as well'.

'I want to give a rational and specific statement about man in his social context,' he has said, expressing himself like a classic documentarist; in contrast to Tarnovetskij, he does not particularize reality or make it poetic. This attitude has appealed to others who have been drawn to the sociological approach to photography. Since his first exhibition he has exhibited as part of a group called 'Four', which also includes Tarnovetskij and the Muscovites Slyusarev and Savelev, all represented in this book.

132–135   From the cycle 'Chernovtsy', 1980–85

Vyacheslav Tarnovetskij (b. 1945), physicist, optics expert, and teacher at various Ukrainian towns, has said that 'there is nothing unphotographic in the world. Just look at things from the right angle and place.' Tarnovetskij lives in Chernovtsy; he and Sergej Lopatyuk form an indivisible couple. He is the older, experienced adviser and teacher but, compared to his pupil, his pictures are provocatively static and strive for poetic effect.

Tarnovetskij has been taking photographs since he was sixteen. From the beginning he admired the lyrical photographs of the Czech Josef Sudek and admits that the Czech quarterly *Revue fotografie* has had a great influence on him, especially in the late 1970s when his current approach to photography was taking shape. As with many other Soviet photographers, it has provoked thought, the search for self-orientation and an independent way of tackling problems.

Tarnovetskij's photographs always represent some minute highlight in everyday human life: two forsaken chairs on the balcony of an old house, closely resembling the mysterious intimacy of a still-life by Sudek; a market place with a single person; a small girl leaving home for an important visit; repairmen stressing the significance of their existence by a funny gesture. A documentary simplicity, but Tarnovetskij pushes his photographs over the boundaries of the documentary genre. He adds the poetry of secrecy, a magical humanity. 'I take photographs of everything because everything is part of my life. And in everything, especially in the most ordinary and commonplace things, the greatest beauty can be discovered.'

136   After the market, 1984
137   Repair brigade, 1984
138   Couple, 1983
139   Beside the sea, 1984

Vladimir Zotov (b. 1932) comes from the village of Aksibayevo in the Tartar Autonomous SSR, but his parents are Russians. He did not take up photography seriously until he was thirty-two, after having tried a number of different jobs. He became a member of the popular amateur photography group TAMSA in Kazan', at the same time enrolling in the faculty of journalism at Kazan' University. His studies and his successful participation in amateur photography – he has appeared in competitions and exhibitions not only in the USSR but also abroad – made it possible for him to turn professional only four years later, when he became a reporter on the staff of the daily Kazan' evening paper.

Zotov is attracted by reportage, a form which he considers uniquely capable of 'catching life in its moments of truth'. Like any other newspaper reporter, he photographs commissioned subjects, which are usually carefully arranged, but in his spare time he keeps strictly to the principle of never interfering with reality and waiting patiently for exactly the right moment. His apprentice period as an amateur and in particular the influence of a group of photographers holding all the traditional opinions concerning photography as a work of art have forced him to improve the aesthetic impact of his pictures. This is why he stresses composition so strongly, even subjugating his subject matter to a particular artistic stance.

Most of his photographs are of life in Kazan', where he now lives, and of life on the Volga. The people in his series about the various workshops of the services enterprise in Kazan' are individual beings radiating an attractive aura of optimism and pleasure in life, thus bringing a cosy atmosphere to their outdated surroundings. This blend of delicate irony and smiling encouragement is characteristic of all Zotov's work. He seems to be emphasizing that the true values of life lie within us and not in our environments. 'Photography is not an art', he says, 'it is a way of perceiving things.'

140   Pioneer camp, from the cycle 'Kazan'', 1981
141   Workshop, from the cycle 'Kazan'', 1981
142   Gorki Street, from the cycle 'Kazan'', 1980
143   By the Volga, from the cycle 'Kazan'', 1981
144   By the Volga, from the cycle 'Kazan'', 1981

The Origins of the New Photography

When in 1929 avant-garde artists from Eastern and Western Europe met for the first time to show a unified front, at the 'Film und Foto' exhibition in Stuttgart, Soviet photography shone with brilliance and exciting beauty. This excitement sprang from its special character. The October Revolution had given it a strictly formulated task: inform, educate, agitate. Photography was turned into a tool of state-controlled agitprop. Yet, although strictly confined to its new social function, it rose to unforeseen heights of creative experimentation.

'Real poetry must by at least one hour be in advance of life' proclaimed the poet Vladimir Mayakovsky after the Revolution. 'It is our duty to experiment,' added his friend the artist Alexander Rodchenko, who, caught up in the spirit of technological progress that marked the age, had discovered the impact photography could have. 'There is nothing revolutionary in the fact that we started to photograph the leaders of the workers in the same way as generals had been photographed during the old régime . . . Everyone knows what to photograph, but only a very few know how . . . We must seek and find, and (rest assured) we shall find, a new aesthetic, together with the enthusiasm and pathos necessary to express our new reality, the Soviet reality, through the medium of photography.'

It was no longer possible to use the old forms of expression. Rodchenko stops taking his 'pictures from the navel', with the camera always in the same position, and starts to show things from new, unusual angles to which he ascribed ideological significance. He tilts the camera to achieve the dynamics of a diagonal composition; reality is made monumental in his photographs by being shot from below and given structural peculiarity by being shot from above; he discovers and gives emotional force to the optimistic effect of large close-ups.

At first the complaint was that this new vision would not be understood by the great mass of people, used only to a straightforwardly descriptive recording of external reality. The first photographic reports after the Revolution had given concise, descriptive, rapid and convincing information and political encouragement to a largely illiterate public. It was not by chance that Lenin considered photography and film to be the most effective tool in the ideological education of the masses. Yet in retrospect it is clear that everyone, including Rodchenko's most vehement opponents among the reporter photographers, eventually set out on the path towards the 'new vision of reality'.

Photography for the state

Military photographers and film groups producing picture news had proved very useful in the Tsar's army and during Kerensky's brief rule and from the beginning Lenin was interested in film and photography. The first decrees concerning nationalization brought both into the service of Soviet power. Two months after the Revolution, film and photography departments were established as part of the State Commission of Peoples' Education. Lectures were held, photography was organized and soon an Institute of Photography was founded in Petrograd. In the autumn of 1918 the government established a special photoreportage department to record current political events. Anyone concealing photographic or film equipment or photographs of the Revolution and its aftermath was punished as severely as someone hiding weapons. Photography became a powerful means of mass communication, a manipulator of public opinion, and an indispensable tool for the control of the masses.

In the countryside, disorganized by the Revolution and Civil War, where even the press had ceased to function for periods, photography played an important role as a witness of events, as a convincing and tangible fragment of reality. It quickly found a place, not only in the show-cases which were placed in the streets of Moscow and Petrograd

Alexander Rodchenko, Photomontage for Vladimir Mayakovsky's poem 'Pro eto', 1923

to provide pictorial information, but also in agitprop trains and boats which travelled the country, in specially published thematic photographic albums and in propaganda posters, often of huge size. The posters, which gave birth to the now classic revolutionary montage and collage, had to include an appealing slogan, a coloured background to attract attention and, above all, photographs.

Thanks to these pictures, Russian peasants in remote villages as well as foreigners thousands of miles from Moscow could see for themselves that the leader of the Revolution, Lenin, was not just a legend but actually living and ruling. His portrait – touched up, as was customary then – was taken as early as January 1918, to fulfil this need for information. The photographer, Moisei Nappelbaum, rapidly went on to create a whole gallery of revolutionary leaders and other significant personalities of his time.

Not every photographer was willing to serve the Soviets. The Revolution and Civil War caused many to leave the country; others kept silent. One reason was that the new conception of photography largely excluded the portrait, the main product of the studios, because it was considered a relic of the bourgeois. For the same reason landscape photography was also neglected. With only a very few exceptions, both these genres disappeared from Soviet photography for many years and even when circumstances became more favourable they never attained the status enjoyed in the photography of other countries. On the other hand photojournalism had a great boom. Required, recognized and appreciated, it remains the dominant trend and determining characteristic of Soviet photography.

But even photojournalism changes. In the first years of Soviet power, and indeed throughout the 1920s, photographers reacted spontaneously to current events. However, in the following years the situation changed. The character of photography became shaped by strict compulsory ideology. Photographers arranged their shots accordingly and even worked to a script. No longer did they instinctively photograph everything that attracted, inspired or surprised them; instead they produced propaganda for the construction programme, which is the central concern of journalism and photojournalism from the end of the 1920s. Gradually they ceased to reflect existing reality, instead creating a pictorial hymn in praise of the work efforts, showing how people should work and live in order to become valid members of socialist society.

Photography thus had a clearly defined social function. It was used mainly in magazines, established from the mid-1920s onwards, either for domestic consumption (*Ogonok* for example) or for the representation of the USSR abroad (such as *USSR under Construction*), which by their appealing propaganda became a specifically Soviet contribution to the early development of world photojournalism. But there were several equally effective exhibitions as, by about 1930, conditions in the country became consolidated – a situation conveyed to the outside world by the efforts of the USSR to be recognized as part of the community of nations. As well as the art and trade exhibitions, such as

Moisei Nappelbaum, The first official portrait of Lenin, 1918

Arkady Shaikhet, People waiting outside M.I. Kalinin's office, Moscow, 1929

M. Alpert, A. Shaikhet and S. Tules, from the essay 'Twenty-four hours in the life of the Filippov family', 1931: Going to work on the tram

'Film und Foto' in Stuttgart in 1929, the International Press Exhibition in Cologne in 1928, or the Russian Exhibition in Zürich in 1929, among many others, there was the sequence of photographs called 'Twenty-four hours in the life of the Filippov family'. Sent as part of a large exhibition to some European capitals in 1931, this showed how to give shape to the propaganda potential of photography to an even greater extent. It consists of a single photo-essay by three photographers – Arkady Shaikhet, Max Alpert and S. Tules – who in seventy-eight pictures told the story of one day in the life of the family of a Moscow labourer, Nikolay Filippov. During this time of economic crisis it had an unprecedented success, which was furthered by its publication in the German weekly *Arbeiter Illustrierte Zeitung*.

In April 1932 the Communist Party issued a resolution on the 'reconstruction of artistic and literary organizations' which substantially affected the development of Soviet culture. The numerous existing artistic organizations were immediately abolished; differences of opinion were expunged in the summer of 1934 by the First Congress of Soviet Writers, which decreed that all Soviet artists should use the methods of socialist realism – that is to say, all their work should correspond to the need to educate the masses in the spirit of socialism. This was not, however, the end of the stormy disputes about the formal aspects of photography, although the nature of the arguments changed somewhat. Criticism of formalism, aestheticism and lack of content reached its peak and the need for access to magazines led all Soviet photographers towards photojournalism.

The great range of Soviet photojournalism includes effective formal devices, employed specifically to give shape and emphasis to the photographed reality. And so the much criticized diagonal composition, which in Soviet Russia was called the 'dynamic diagonal', sharply tilted views from below or above, and large close-ups also appear in the photographs of Max Alpert, Semyon Fridlyand, Arkady Shaikhet, Georgy Petrusov, Georgy Zelma and others who originally had nothing in common with the experimentation of Rodchenko, El Lissitzky or Boris Ignatovitch. Together they created a new sort of photojournalism, in which the photograph illustrates the happy future and shows the path toward it.

Photographing the war

World War II, which for the Soviet Union began with the invasion by Nazi Germany in 1941, opened a new chapter in Soviet photography. As in the days of the Revolution and the years that followed, a dramatic reality forced photographers to spontaneous and personally involved statements. Photography again acquired a new vitality. War, bringing suffering at the front and at home, had an impact on everyone without distinction.

More than two hundred professional photographers from agencies, newspapers and magazines enlisted. Like their journalist colleagues they put on a uniform on the first

Georgy Zelma, On Red Square, 1931

Alexander Rodchenko, Sportsmen parade on Red Square, Moscow, 1932

Max Alpert, The construction of the Fergana canal, 1939

Dmitri Baltermanas, On the road of war, 1941

day of war and, if they survived, did not take it off until the war was over. They stayed with the front line throughout the advance on Berlin. Unique photographic testimonies were produced, like Boris Kudoiarov's extensive essay on nine hundred days in the life of the people of Leningrad. Others, equally strong and emotional, were created by Michail Trachman on the flight of the partisans and the resistance of civilians in the rear, who lived underground in the so-called 'zemliankas' (trenches); by Alexander Uzlian on the fierce attacks by sailors from the feared Black Sea fleet; by the woman reporter Galina Sanko on the sufferings of homeless children freely wandering the countryside; by Dmitri Baltermanas on the crimes perpetrated by the Nazis on the people of occupied Kerch.

But no photographers of the war stand out as better than the others; the best work of them all achieves an equal passion. Perhaps the fact that they were so strongly involved in events helped them to capture emotion while yet preserving respect and restraint in their approach to human suffering. Their cameras are not intrusive, although shots tend to be close-ups achieved without the use of telephoto lenses. 'War is above all grief' said Dmitri Baltermanas, today the best-known Soviet war photographer, involuntarily expressing what it was that often led photographers, regardless of their newspaper assignments and despite possible reprisal for devoting attention to forbidden subjects, intuitively to photograph what they saw or felt. From profound personal experiences they were able to produce what today is regarded as the most noteworthy achievement in Soviet war photography – pictures of emotions.

It was the war photography that drew the world's attention to Soviet photography as a whole. Just as *War and Peace*, half a century after Napoleon's Russian campaign, had enraptured the world by its clear picture of the universal character of the defence of the country, World War II as portrayed by Soviet photographers has, several decades later, captured the world's imagination by its creative force and has evoked a desire for greater knowledge. Until then Soviet photography was not mentioned in histories of photography and Soviet photographers appeared in no dictionaries or manuals. True, the history of Soviet photography was written by Sergej Morozov in the 1950s, in a book which dealt with Russian photography from its beginnings, but this was not read abroad; it was confined to the ideology of the Stalinist era. Also unknown outside Russia is the series of books by Leonid Volkov-Lannit, published in the late 1960s and early 1970s, which covers the history of the photography of the Revolution.

Postwar photography

What happened to that personal involvement, that passion, of the war photography? What became of that raw directness which it shared with photography of the immediate post-Revolution period? History repeated itself, and instead of embarking on a new era of candid, realist photography with a humanist accent, like that emerging in the rest of the world, Soviet photography after the trauma of the war, which had shaken the schematic 1930s model of photography, returned to the place where its development had been severed – to a simplified vision of life, to the illustration of externals. Everyone is happy and laughing and with great optimism participates in the work of construction. It is as if there were no burned-out towns or villages without men, taken from their women by the war; as if there were no barren fields or industrial plants razed to the ground, the reconstruction of which meant great hardship and sacrifice and necessarily profoundly affected the lives of the people, just as they had been affected by the war. There are, none the less, powerful photographic testimonies from that period, and the archives will one day show them to the world, just as they revealed after an interval of many years the photographs of the post-Revolution and war periods.

The rapid postwar development of the Soviet photography industry has been accompanied by a large amateur movement; thousands gather in school or factory clubs, in town and village cultural centres, in dozens of national studios. The same had been the case, to a lesser extent, in the prewar period. Photography has become one of the most popular hobbies. This activity is a natural hatching-place for talent, and from it well-known photojournalists arose in the 1960s, providing new blood for Soviet photojournalism. Unlike their predecessors, these young photographers had received a good training in the highly developed amateur movement. They established a healthy challenge to the fossilized traditions of photojournalism, and were quickly given opportunities to work for important newspapers and magazines. For example, in the weekly *Ogonok*, under the guidance of its chief reporter, the veteran war correspondent Dmitri Baltermanas, such photographers as Gennadi Koposov, Lev Sherstennikov and Alexander Nagralian turned into sophisticated and sensitive story-tellers. In the agencies APN and TASS, in the magazine *Sovietski soiuz*, in the newspaper *Izvestia* and elsewhere they were joined by others of similar character – Juri Abramochkin, Viktor Achlomov and Valeri Gende-Rote.

This development in the new generation also reflects the influence of the 20th Congress of the Communist Party of the USSR, which in 1956, three years after Stalin's death, analysed the preceding period of schematism and assessed the detrimental consequences of the personality cult. This influence can be observed even more strongly in the least expected place, although from the historical and political point of view it is the logical place: in the Baltic countries. Lithuania, Latvia and Estonia began to demonstrate through photography their own unique, rich cultural tradition, their individual means of expression and their right to self-determination. Photographs of Lithuania gave rise to the idea of organizing photography and an official state-subsidized Society for Creative Photography of the Lithuanian SSR was established, creating an opportunity for unprecedented photographic activities.

The Baltic photographers

Photography had long-established roots in the Baltic republics. It was in the university of the Lithuanian town of Vilnius that Jan Bulhak in 1919 founded a department of photography (of which he was professor), one of the first in any European university. In the Baltic countries arose artistic personalities who were to be of great importance for the whole Russian revolutionary avant-garde – like, for example, the Latvian Gustav Klucis. The Baltic Soviet Republics, especially Lithuania, have since the 1960s brought new blood to the whole of Soviet photography. Opposed to the rigid official clichés, they have introduced into photography a fresh look at the ordinary life of ordinary people. Against the generally accepted view of an age of science and technology, they set the force of the traditional links between man and nature, of a harmony that alone gives meaning to life. They show folk customs, the ancient strength of human community, the special beauty of the rugged country by the seashore, the charm of the way of life of ancient towns. Although in total it is a romanticized image of an ideal, nevertheless it does portray the health and joy that come from a simple and wise philosophy of life. So Lithuanian photography, and Baltic photography as a whole, is actually a specifically Soviet expression of humanistic postwar photography, whose creed was an optimistic view of life and belief in the goodness of man. This development, which was a break with existing photographic rigidity, took the form of an aestheticization of expression. Frequent use was made of wide-angle lenses, which with their ability to distort give the pictures a highly dramatic character. Even the smallest detail becomes important and the commonplace appears exceptional.

The struggle of the Baltic photographers for self-expression and recognition was not easy, but their ascendancy was so strong and unstoppable, and gained so many followers in the other Soviet republics, that finally they succeeded. While other Soviet photographers are still organized only in the photographic section of the Union of Journalists of the USSR, or in the amateur movement, the Lithuanian photographers, thanks to the Society for Creative Photography, have the opportunity to exhibit regularly, to publish photographs in annuals, to organize seminars and festivals and to create galleries and museums of photography. Photographic activity in Latvia and Estonia has developed similarly, although not on quite such a large scale. And so paradoxically Baltic photography in the 1960s – and throughout much of the 1970s as well – practically came to represent Soviet photography as a whole. Both within the Soviet Union and, thanks to its good organization, abroad, it attracts both publicity and respect. Not surprisingly, a number of the young generation of photographers in other parts of the country acknowledge the Baltic photographers as a source of inspiration, as advisers and

174

Valeri Gende-Rote, Yuri Gagarin,
14 April 1961

Lev Assanov,
A merry weaver,
1965

Gennadi Koposov, Minus 55°C, 1971

as teachers. It was in the Baltic countries that questions of independently organized platforms for photography and professional photographic training were tackled, as was the need to work with theory, criticism and history.

There is another source of inspiration frequently acknowledged by contemporary Soviet photographers – the Czechoslovak quarterly photographic *Revue fotografie*, published in Prague since 1957, which appears in both Czech and in a large Russian edition for circulation in the Soviet Union. The only Soviet photographic magazine is the monthly *Sovetskoye foto*, which is addressed largely to the general public interested in photography. The *Revue* is aimed at those with a more serious interest, and has responded to new trends, has developed thinking about photography, and has even exceeded the usual bounds of the subject, moving into other fields in which photography has found a place. In the 1970s especially it provided the impulse towards perceiving photography not simply as pictures, but also as language. This helped to introduce a new type of photographer. It was the first to publish the Baltic photographers and gradually became the platform for numerous other Soviet photographers, many of whom first learned of each other's work through its pages.

The new photography

What, then, does current Soviet photography look like and who are the photographers who appeared in the 1970s and 80s? They are a group of educated and sensitive artists, scientists and technicians – the young Soviet intelligentsia, who find in photography a means of self-expression. Many have left their original professions to work as photographers, usually as freelances. This is a new tendency in Soviet photography, and until recently an uncommon one. Photography produced as independent creativity is a form of self-expression, no matter how the photographers make their living, and such an approach represents a new stage in the development of Soviet photography, introducing completely new qualities – personal philosophy in particular. Thus, while the illustrative type of magazine photograph is still the sort of work produced by most photographers both professional and amateur, and while the courageous breakthrough of the Baltic photographers has, with few exceptions, not yet advanced beyond its initial targets, this photography is brimful of the need to have its say about contemporary life and, on the basis of an analysis and cognition of reality, to express the feelings of people which derive from the time and place in which they live.

This photography does not long for the public display, honours and recognition to which the Baltic photographers had naturally once aspired. Now it is a private need. It thus also seems to be modest, conducting a dialogue between reality and the emotions which reality inspires. Its state-ments have many meanings and are wide open to various interpretations, for the reality shown in the photograph has always had an inner dimension, a meaning concealed between the lines. This is photography with an instinct for combined meanings, for slight shifts in significance, for absurdity, gentle irony and the truth revealed by acute sensibility. It is honest photography. It accurately and sensitively reflects the opinions and attitudes to life of people in the 1970s and 80s. In that lies its new social involvement.

'When I pressed the shutter release of my camera for the first time, I knew at once that photography would stay with me for the rest of my life,' said Lyalya Kuznetsova, a civil engineer from Tartary and a brilliant talent, intuitively led by feeling and experience to the very essence of human values and their real meaning. A similar attitude was expressed by Boris Savelev, an aeronautic expert; by Aleksandr Slyusarev, an interpreter; by Sergej Lopatyuk and Vyacheslav Tarnovetskij, university lecturers; by Elena Darikovich, a former laboratory assistant; and by Vladimir Siomin, a reporter. They are not attracted by organized photographic life, even that of the Baltic region, still an ideal for many photographers and several national photographic studios. They tend to associate freely, according to whether their opinions coincide or whether they feel drawn to one another. Regardless of their origins – the Ukraine, the Baltic, Tartary or Russia – they call themselves 'The Seventies', because it was during that decade, in which most of them first took up photography, that they achieved individual expression and their own photographic style. If we add to them those established photographers whose work is a stimulus and inspiration for the new generation, we can discern the shape of contemporary Soviet photography.

Aleksandras Matsiyauskas, from the cycle 'The beach', 1981–2

Bibliography

Note on the introduction

Timothy Ware's book *The Orthodox Church* (Harmondsworth, 1963 and repr.) provides the best available guide to Lyalya Kuznetsova's worshippers. The pictures in this book might be looked at in conjunction with a reading of recent Soviet literature. Eduard Gladkov's villagers look like neighbours and relations of those described in the short stories of Vasily Shukshin, some of which appear in *Roubles in Words, Kopeks in Figures* (London, 1985). Yuri Trifonov, in *The House on the Embankment* (London, 1985), writes about a Moscow which can also be sensed in the photographs of Elena Darikovich and Boris Savelev. For a range of recent Soviet writing in translation see *Contemporary Russian Prose*, edited by Carl and Ellendea Proffer (Ann Arbor, Michigan, 1982). Comparisons between photography and literature are hazardous, but Soviet writers reflect on memories of the war, on relations between the city and the country, and on much which is pertinent to these photographs.

I.J.

The origins of the new photography

Alexandrov, A. and Šajchet, A., *Arkadij Shaikchet* (Moscow, 1973)

Bòltjanskij, G., *Očerki po istoriji fotografii v SSSR [Studies in the History of Photography in the USSR]* (Moscow, 1939)

Burjak, Igor, *Georgi Lipskerova* (Moscow, 1976)

Dyko, Lidia, *Boris Kudojarov* (Moscow, 1975)

Evgenov, S., *Abram Sterenberg* (Moscow, 1941)

Glaeser, E., and Weiskopf, F.C., *The Land Without Unemployment: Three Years of the Five Year Plan* (London, 1931)

Karginov, German, *Rodcsenko* (Budapest, 1975)

Karmen, Roman, *Max Alpert* (Moscow, 1974)

Lavrentjev, Alexandr, *Alexandr Rodtschenko: Possibilities of Photography* (Cologne, 1982)

Linhart, Lubomir, *Aleksandr Rodčenko* (Prague, 1960)

Lissitzky-Küppers, Sophie, *El Lissitzky* (Dresden, 1967; English translation, London, 1968)

Morozov, Sergej, *Russkaja khudožestvennaja fotografija [Russian Artistic Photography]* (Moscow, 1955)

—— *Sovetskaja khudožestvennaja fotografija [Soviet Artistic Photography]* (Moscow, 1958)

Morozova, Saava, *Galina Sanko* (Moscow, 1975)

Mrázková, Daniela and Remeš, Vladimír, *Fotografovali válku sovětská válečná fotoreportáž 1941–1945* (Prague, 1975); translated into English as *The Russian War: 1941–1945* (New York, 1977, and London, 1978) and into German as *Von Moskau nach Berlin, Der Krieg im Osten* (Oldenburg and Munich, 1979)

—— 'Soviet photography between the World Wars, 1917–41', *Camera*, 1981, No. 6

—— *Die Sowjetunion zwischen den Kriegen 1917–1941* (Oldenburg and Munich, 1981)

—— *Early Soviet Photographers*, the catalogue of an exhibition at the Museum of Modern Art, Oxford, 1982

Oginskaja, L., *Gustav Klucis* (Moscow, 1981)

Peskov, Vasili, *Dmitrij Baltermanas* (Moscow, 1977)

Shudakov, Grigory, *Pioneers of Soviet Photography* (London, 1984)

Remeš, Vladimír, *Kurským dělníkům, fotomontáže Jurije Rožkova [To the Workers of Kursk: Photomontages by Jurije Rožkova]* (Prague, 1982)

Vartanov, Anri, *Georgij Petrusov* (Moscow, 1979)

Vilemkon, B., *Georgij Zelma* (Moscow, 1978)

Volkov-Lannit, L.F., *Alexandr Rodčenko risujet, fotografirujet, sporrit [Alexander Rodchenko Draws, Photographs, Discusses]* (Moscow, 1969)

—— *Istorija pišetsja objektivom [History is Written with a Lens]* (Moscow, 1971)

Weiss, Evelyn, *Alexandr Rodtschenko 1920–1938* (Cologne, 1978)

Reference works

Contemporary Photographers (London and New York, 1982)

Mrázková, Daniela, *The Story of Photography* (Prague, 1985)

Periodicals

Revue fotografie (Prague, 1957–78)

Sovetskoye foto (Moscow, 1956–)